FX FACES

by SNAZAROO

KINGfISHER

Contents

Introduction   5
Materials   6
Ageing the Face   8
Grandad   8
Count Dracula and His Bride   10
Shaping the Face   12
Horrible Hag   12
Boily Face   14
Pirates Ahoy!   16
Fantastic Fish   18
Changing the Hair   20
The Wizard   22
Mad Scientist   24
False Parts   26
Brainy Aliens   26
Flaky Face   28
Three-Eyed Ghoul   30
Gallery   32

▶ *To paint this witch: Apply a light green base with a sponge. Paint in dark green around the eyes and mouth, in the hollows of the cheeks and along the frown lines. Add the black outlines and white highlights with a fine brush. Finish off with a thin line of red under the eyes.*

Introduction

Have you ever wondered how a professional make-up artist can turn ordinary-looking actors into terrifying monsters or aliens or make them look as though they have been injured in an accident? This book will show you how to create some fabulous special effects using make-up and materials that are easily obtained and simple to use. If you are new to face painting, take time to look at the four step-by-step photographs of the green monster below before you try more difficult faces. These show you the basic techniques of applying water-based face paint with a sponge and brush.

Hair can be coloured with face paints, too.

Always apply the base coat first.

1 Cover the whole face with green paint using a slightly damp sponge. Add a second coat if necessary to strengthen the colour.

Fabric shapes sewn on a black skirt.

▲ *A costume can make all the difference when creating a really effective character. It's a good idea to start a collection of fabric, clothing, wigs and accessories to go with your face-painting designs.*

Paint outlines of larger shapes first then infill with colour.

Apply one colour at a time.

2 Paint in the red eyebrows with a large brush. Then add red markings on the cheeks and beside the eyes.

Paint lighter colours over darker ones.

Add dark or black outlines last.

3 Paint sharp white fangs at the sides of the mouth then add a flash of white to the corner of each eyebrow.

4 Outline the nostrils, lips and fangs in black. Add spiky black eyebrows and finish off with black spots all over the face.

Materials

Glitter creams are a fun extra and great for fantasy faces.

Today, you can buy all kinds of exciting special-effects materials and a range of bright face-painting colours. You should be able to find face paints in most toy and craft shops. Make sure that they are the sort that wash off with water. Avoid greasy stick make-up that is hard to remove from faces and clothes. If you have a lot of materials, store them in an airtight box or buy a special carrying case.

▲ *A good selection of colours, several sponges and a range of different-sized brushes is essential.*

A BASIC FX FACE-PAINTING KIT includes a set of water-based face paints, three or four brushes and sponges, a towel to wrap around your model's neck, a container for water, some special-effects wax, a stipple sponge, a plastic spatula, crêpe hair, a bald cap and some fake blood.

Plastic balls used to create alien heads (see page 26).

◀ *Bald caps can be bought from a special theatrical supplier or a joke shop. Thin caps are more effective than thick ones but are more expensive.*

▲ *Crêpe hair is made of wool. It comes in tightly woven braids in many natural hair colours.*

▶ *A stipple sponge is used to texture face paint or wax. Special-effects wax can be moulded into false noses or used as a light adhesive. Fake blood comes in a gel or liquid. Use it carefully though – it can stain clothes.*

▼*Always keep your pots, brushes and towels scrupulously clean and change the water regularly.*

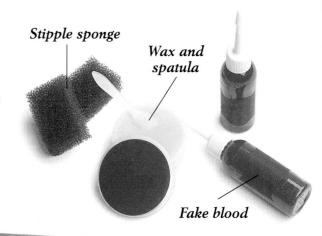

Stipple sponge

Wax and spatula

Fake blood

Ageing the Face

Base coat should match model's skin colour.

1 Apply a light brown base coat over the whole face with a dry sponge, then paint on the white highlights with a brush.

Once you know how to apply basic face paints you can start to practise the special-effects technique of ageing a face. This is the first skill taught in make-up school, and it involves an understanding of bone structure, shading and highlighting. It's not as hard as it sounds and it will help you to make your characters much more realistic.

Paint the ears, too.

2 Deepen the wrinkles and shade around the eyes and cheeks and down the sides of the nose in grey.

Grandad

TO AGE A FACE, start by studying your own reflection in a mirror. Screw up your face to see where wrinkle lines will appear when you get older. Feel the sunken areas around your eyes and the hollows of your cheeks. Then feel where the bones are more prominent – your forehead, nose, chin and cheekbones. When ageing a face, you need to shade the sunken areas and highlight the more prominent areas.

Paint thin red lines in the lips.

Sponge white paint into the hair.

Whiten the eyebrows with a brush.

3 Blend the areas of white and grey with a dry sponge, then dab red on the cheeks with a stipple sponge for broken veins.

4 For a more unkempt appearance, dab a little dark brown face paint over the forehead, cheeks and chin with a dry sponge.

▶ *Grandad is wearing an old tweed jacket and woolly scarf. You could also add spectacle frames with the glass removed.*

8

If necessary, darken the hair with black paint and paint in a V-shaped hairline with a brush.

COUNT DRACULA AND HIS BRIDE

◀ *Buy or make a large black cape for Dracula. His bride is wearing a long white dress and a veil made from an old lacy net curtain attached to a piece of elastic.*

DRACULA IS THE MOST FAMOUS VAMPIRE of all time and is a popular character for parties, particularly at Halloween. Both these faces have been created using the ageing techniques described on the previous page. Add a smudge of red paint under the eyes to make them appear bloodshot and use a fine brush to paint on the feathery eyebrows. Finish off by adding white fangs outlined in black. We've painted a touch of red on the tips of the fangs or you could use a few drops of fake blood instead.

▶ *To paint Count Dracula's skull-like companion, apply a white base, sponge on pale yellow and purple for a textured effect, then add the black patches. (See page 2 for a larger picture to follow.)*

Dab red on the cheeks with a stipple sponge.

Shaping the Face

Make-up artists use special wax or nose putty to change the shape of a nose, add pointed ears or chins or to create bags under the eyes. Wax is great fun to use and extremely versatile. It can be also be used to create scars and wounds or even as a light adhesive. The best kind of wax to buy is one that will stick directly on to clean, dry skin but will wash off easily in warm water. When you want to remove the wax, scrape most of it off with your fingers then wash away the rest. You may need to use cleansing cream to remove oil-based wax.

▲ *Practise a range of different nose shapes – a hooked nose as shown above, a bumpy monster nose or a turned-up pixie nose.*

◀ *To complete the character, we've added a wig but have put it on upside down. Find out more about wigs on page 20.*

Horrible Hag

OUR SCARY HAG has a hooked nose complete with wart. The wart is simply a piece of breakfast cereal, stuck to the side of the nose with a tiny piece of wax. Once you have shaped the nose, apply your face paint. Here, we've sponged on a green base coat, brushed a little red under the eyes and added black feathery eyebrows.

1 Soften a small piece of wax between your fingers, roll it into a ball and position it on the centre of the nose.

2 Mould the wax into shape with your fingers or with a spatula, then smooth the edges on to the skin.

Boily Face

HERE, **SPECIAL-EFFECTS WAX** has been applied all over the face to create an effective ghoul with nasty green boils. When applying the wax, make sure you smooth down the edges so that it will stick to the skin. Once the wax has been on the skin for a while, it will get warmer and begin to wrinkle, giving the surface more texture. You can use wax to shape the face in other ways. Try designing a new character with a thick ridge running right across the eyebrows or with a wide bulbous nose.

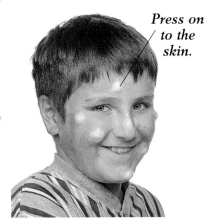

Press on to the skin.

Cobweb hair bought from a joke shop.

1 Soften about eight small balls of wax between your fingers and position the balls all over the face.

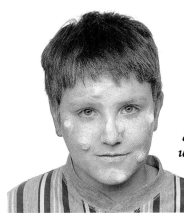

Paint in ageing lines with a brush.

2 Dab on a pale green base coat with a sponge or thick brush. Apply several coats to build up the colour.

3 Sponge purple paint over the wax boils and add patches of dark green around the eyes, nose and chin.

14

With a brush, paint dark grey circles around the eyes and long grooves from the nose to the corners of the mouth.

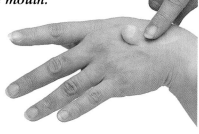

1 Apply small balls of wax to the backs of the hands in the same way that you did for the face.

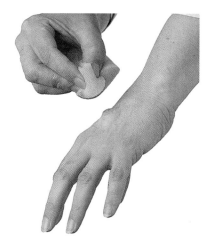

2 Dab colour over the wax with a sponge, as before. It's advisable to paint only the backs of the hands or the tops of the feet, not the palms or the soles, for obvious reasons!

◀ *When creating a character like this don't forget other parts of the body that may be showing. Hands and feet can easily be painted to match the rest of the disguise.*

Paint black lines over the lips to make them look cracked.

◀ *This boily ghoul is wearing a simple black hood decorated with long strands of pale cobweb hair.*

Pirates Ahoy!

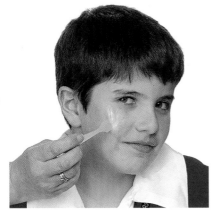

Leave wax in a raised ridge.

1 Soften a small piece of wax between your fingers, mould it into a sausage shape then position it on the cheek.

2 Use a plastic spatula or a similar blunt tool to make a groove running down the whole length of the wax.

Paint on fake blood with a fine brush.

3 Apply red and black paint with a stipple sponge to create a bruising effect, then paint on the fake blood with a fine brush.

IN ACTION AND ADVENTURE FILMS or when making a television drama about hospitals, the make-up artist is often asked to create realistic injuries and scars. With just a little special-effects wax and some fake blood, you can create wounds that will send your friends rushing to the first-aid box. Take extra care when using theatrical blood because it may stain clothes. If you don't want to use fake blood, you can apply red face paint instead. However, it won't look quite so effective.

Let a little fake blood dribble down the cheek.

▶ *Sponge a thin coat of light brown over the face once you have created the wounds. The girl pirate's face has been aged slightly using dark brown shading and the techniques described on page 8. Paint over the eyebrows in black and, for an unshaven look, dab a little black paint around the chin with a stipple sponge.*

16

Headscarves and bright waistcoats complete the pirate disguise.

Paint on a thin black moustache.

Fantastic Fish

THIS **FANTASTIC FISH** has been created by sticking paper scales (here, torn out of ordinary kitchen paper towels) to the face with a thin layer of special-effects wax. The scales have then been sponged with orange water-based face paint. When applying face paint to paper, you need to make your sponge much wetter than usual because the paper absorbs a lot of water. Keep the paint thick and apply more coats if you find that the colour looks thin. Use wax and torn paper to create other amazing creatures, such as a green scaly dragon.

If you don't have a wig, sponge green paint into the hair and backcomb it (see page 20).

Gloss the lips or paint in pink.

Tie back long hair.

Keep the layer of wax thin.

Press gently until it sticks.

Dab on the paint so that you don't tear the paper.

1 Soften a small amount of special-effects wax between your fingers and smooth it over the forehead and cheekbones. Work quickly so the wax doesn't dry out.

2 Have plenty of torn paper scales ready before you apply the wax. Lay the scales over the wax, slightly overlapping each one.

3 Dab orange face paint over the paper scales with a sponge, taking the paint over the cheeks and forehead.

Add a green or blue wig to complete the fishy look.

▼ *To create this costume, long thin strips of tulle, net and shiny fabric have been attached to a collar made out of large satin fish scales.*

4 Paint around the eyes in pale blue then outline the scales in the same colour. Add touches of silver glitter for extra sparkle.

Changing the Hair

To make a character look really complete you shouldn't forget to pay attention to the hair. Hair can be slicked back with hair gel, painted with water-based face paints or sprayed with coloured or glitter hairspray. It's also worth starting a collection of wigs and hairpieces (lengths of hair that are fixed to the model's hair with hairpins). On the next page, you can find out how to use crêpe hair to make a moustache and beard.

▲ *Metallic glitter wigs like these are available in many costume shops and are not expensive to buy. They come in a wide range of colours and are good for fantasy faces.*

▶ *Paint hair with water-based face paints using a damp sponge or large brush. The lighter the hair colour, the more vibrant the colour will become. Water-based face paints will wash out easily with shampoo.*

Coloured hairspray (When using hairspray, always shield the eyes.)

◀ *Buy a few cheap wigs from a costume shop or hunt through jumble sales. You can colour old wigs with hairspray or re-cut them to create a new wild style.*

▼ *A wild character needs a wild hairstyle. To make long hair wild and tangled, hold it in small sections and run a fine-toothed comb through it backwards, pushing strands of hair up towards the scalp. Here, we've tied in ribbons and strips of net and shiny gauze to complete the effect.*

Colour the hair with white water-based face paint to match the beard.

WE'VE USED WHITE CREPE HAIR to create this wizard's long, flowing moustache and beard. Crêpe hair comes in different shades of tightly crimped woollen strands that are wound into a long plait. You can attach crêpe hair to clean, dry skin with wax or with a water-soluble spirit gum (a liquid adhesive used by many professional make-up artists). If you use spirit gum, test it on a small skin patch first – it may cause irritation.

◀ *Paint your wizard's face with a fantasy design. Here, we've used bright colours and bold, sweeping brushstrokes.*

1 Sponge on a base coat then smooth a thin layer of wax just under the nose and over the chin. Gently pat the wax with your fingers to make it tacky so that the hair will easily stick to it.

Comb through the beard then cut it into a point once it has been fixed in position.

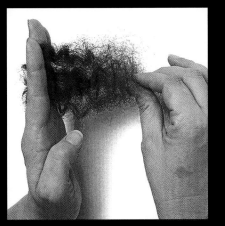

2 Cut the hair into appropriate lengths and gently separate the coiled strands to make four or five thin layers. Mix different colours for a more natural look.

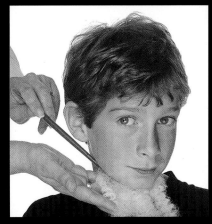

3 Attach each layer of hair, starting from the bottom of the chin and working upwards. Use the end of a brush to tease the hair into place.

23

Mad Scientist

Cut cap over ears.

1 Sponge yellow all over the face. If you are using a white or skin-coloured bald cap, paint that, too.

OUR MAD SCIENTIST has turned a strange colour and has lost most of his hair in his last experiment... This effect looks professional but is actually very easy to do. It uses crêpe hair again (here, dark brown) and a bald cap. We used a thin yellow swimming cap for this character but you can also buy special latex or plastic caps from a theatrical stockist or joke shop.

Thinner caps look better than thick ones but they are more expensive and can tear. Once the bald cap is in position, trim off any excess plastic around the forehead and ears with scissors.

Dab paint over natural eyebrows.

Use a little at a time.

Water-soluble spirit gum

2 Using a sponge, shade in the area around the eyes, the hollows of the cheeks and the chin with brown.

4 Attach crêpe hair to the cap layer by layer, as shown on page 23, using water-soluble spirit gum or wax. Once the crêpe hair is in position, gently comb it through.

Stick eyebrows on the cap, not the skin.

Attach the sideburns to the cap just in front of the ears.

Sponge paint on the hands to match.

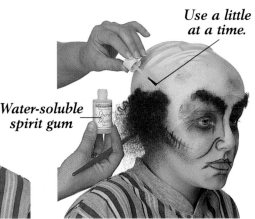

3 Use a fine brush to outline the eyes and lips and add wrinkles. Attach crêpe hair eyebrows and sideburns with spirit gum or wax.

▶ *The mad scientist is wearing an old tweed jacket and a woollen scarf. Characters created with bald caps look fun but remember that if you wear a bald cap to a party, it can get hot and uncomfortable after a while.*

False Parts

Adding false parts to your characters can look really effective. Make-up artists in films and television create some amazing special effects using liquid plastics that are painted directly on the skin, or by giving actors specially-made false body parts. On this and the next two pages we'll show you how you can create some really simple effects at home, using a lightweight ball and some easy-to-make gelatin skin.

▲ *Here, we're painted the ball, face and ears green, the lips pink, and have used black to shade the head and face and outline the lips and eyes.*

Brainy Aliens

THESE ALIEN HEADS are lightweight balls with large holes cut into them so that they sit on the head. On the green alien, the ball has been cut to shape over the forehead and sits just above the eyebrows. The orange head has been cut into a point between the eyebrows. Stick some foam strips just inside the ball for comfort.

▶ *Apply an orange base all over with a sponge and blend in red at the sides of the face. Paint in the green and black patches around the forehead, cheeks and chin with a wide brush, then add the bands over the eyes, following the shape of the eyebrows. Paint the white teeth over your model's mouth and outline in black.*

▼ *Our alien's tunic is made from long strips of torn coloured fabric attached to an elastic collar.*

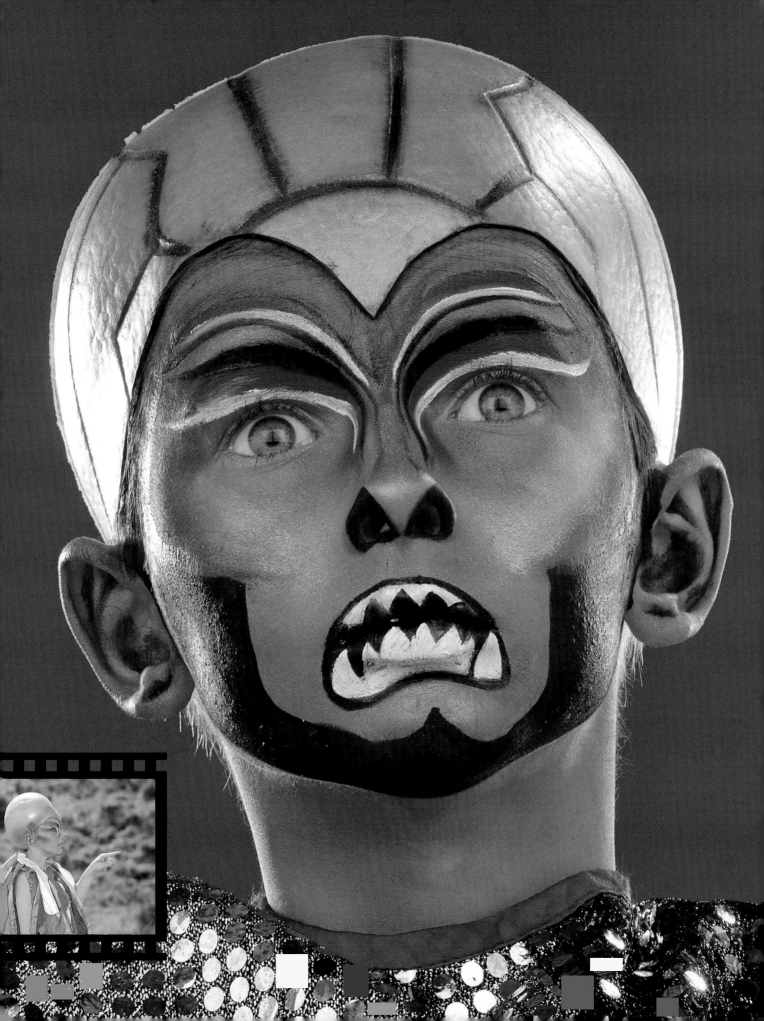

Flaky Face

TO MAKE FALSE SKIN, you simply need to heat gelatin and glycerin with a little water (see the recipe below). Gelatin can be bought in supermarkets and glycerin from a chemist. Make-up artists call this 'skin gel' and they use it to make all kinds of effects, including realistic-looking burns. Here, we've used it to create a face with flaking skin.

▶ *Complete the character by adding dark green shading around the eyes, nose and mouth. Brush purple below the eyes and add a few drops of fake blood or red paint.*

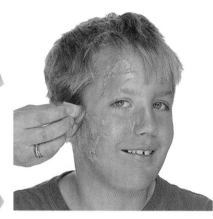

1 Dip a piece of false skin into a cup of hot water for 30 seconds and check that it has become slightly tacky. Position the false skin on to the face, smooth side down. It will immediately stick. Once the false skin is in position, dab on your base coat with a sponge.

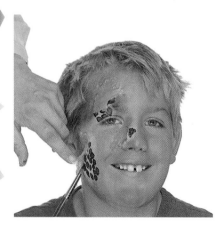

2 Gently peel back some of the false skin and paint a design underneath. Here, we've painted a reptile skin in yellow and green.

How to Make False Skin*

1 *Put three heaped tablespoons of gelatin and two tablespoons of glycerin into a saucepan and add enough water to make the mixture the consistency of mashed potato.*

2 *Gently heat the mixture until all the glycerin has dissolved into a liquid and you can pour it off a spoon.*

3 *Cover a tray or wooden board with clingfilm and paint the mixture on to the film in patches or strips, depending on what size and shape you want the false skin to be. When set, gently peel the skin from the clingfilm.*

* Not recommended for children under 12 without adult supervision.

Three-Eyed Ghoul

Red paint or fake blood completes this gnoulish character.

FALSE EYES can be bought from a joke shop and can look horribly realistic. They are easily stuck to the face with a little special-effects wax. The false eye on this face was made using the recipe for false skin on page 28. To make a good eye shape, pour the mixture into an egg cup and leave it to set for a couple of hours. Once set, scoop the eye out of the cup. Stick the flat side to the face with wax and paint the rounded side with ordinary face paints, as shown in the photographs. This can be done before or after the eye is fixed in position.

▶ *Sponge light grey over the whole face then pink on the forehead, eyes and cheeks. Darken the eyebrows with black and add shadows under the eyes. Outline the nostrils, then paint in the black-and-white mouth.*

Smooth down the edges with your fingers.

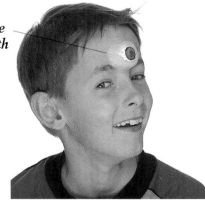

1 Making sure that the skin is clean and dry, fix the eye in the centre of the forehead with special-effects wax.

2 Build up the edges of the false eye with wax to make a socket. This will also help to keep the eye firmly in place.

Gallery

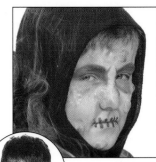

Amy Wigglesworth

THE PUBLISHERS would like to thank the models – who look very different without their make-up – and face painters Lauren Staton, Wilhelmina Barnden and Jacqueline Russon.

Amy Wigglesworth

Lee Lamber

Scott Lamber

Luke Lamber

Patrick Milburn

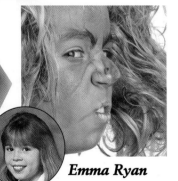

Emma Ryan

Jack Husebo

Colin Capp

KINGFISHER
An imprint of Kingfisher Publications Plc
New Penderel House, 283-288 High Holborn
London WC1V 7HZ
First published by Kingfisher Publications Plc 1997
10 9 8 7 6 5 4 3 2
Copyright © In-Resort Services Ltd 1997
All rights reserved.
A CIP catalogue record for this book
is available from the British Library.
ISBN 0 7534 0110 X
Editor: Sue Nicholson
Designer: Smiljka Surla
Photographer: Roger Crump

If you can't find any of the materials mentioned in this book, write to us for a mail order catalogue at:

Snazaroo,
Unit 1A-1D Brunel Way,
Mart Road Industrial
Estate, Minehead,
Somerset TA24 5BJ,
United Kingdom.

Printed in Hong Kong

Luke Freeman